PATCHWORK ISLAND

PATCHWORK ISLAND

BY KARLA KUSKIN

ILLUSTRATED BY PETRA MATHERS

HarperCollins *Publishers*

Patchwork Island
Text copyright © 1994 by Karla Kuskin
Illustrations copyright © 1994 by Petra Mathers
Printed in the U.S.A. All rights reserved.

Library of Congress Cataloging-in-Publication Data
Kuskin, Karla.
  Patchwork island / by Karla Kuskin ; illustrated by Petra Mathers.
      p.   cm.
  Summary: A mother making a quilt for her child stitches the varied
topography of their beautiful island into her patchwork pattern.
  ISBN 0-06-021242-X. — ISBN 0-06-021284-5 (lib. bdg.)
  1. Quilts—Juvenile poetry.   2. Children's poetry, American.
[1. Quilts—Poetry.   2. American poetry.]   I. Mathers, Petra, ill.
II. Title.
PS3561.U79P38 1994   92-10344
811'.54—dc20   CIP
                                                             AC

Typography by Christine Kettner
1   2   3   4   5   6   7   8   9   10   ❖
First Edition

This book is Jool's
    — K. K.

For Andrea and Magic
    — P. M.

This place began with yellow, green and blue, a little red,

needles, scissors, thread.

A clever mother stitched the colors up.

The green for leaves and fields, blue water

and the red that shades to brown

for roads that wander down green valleys over

yellow hills and end like ribbons cut along the edge of blue.

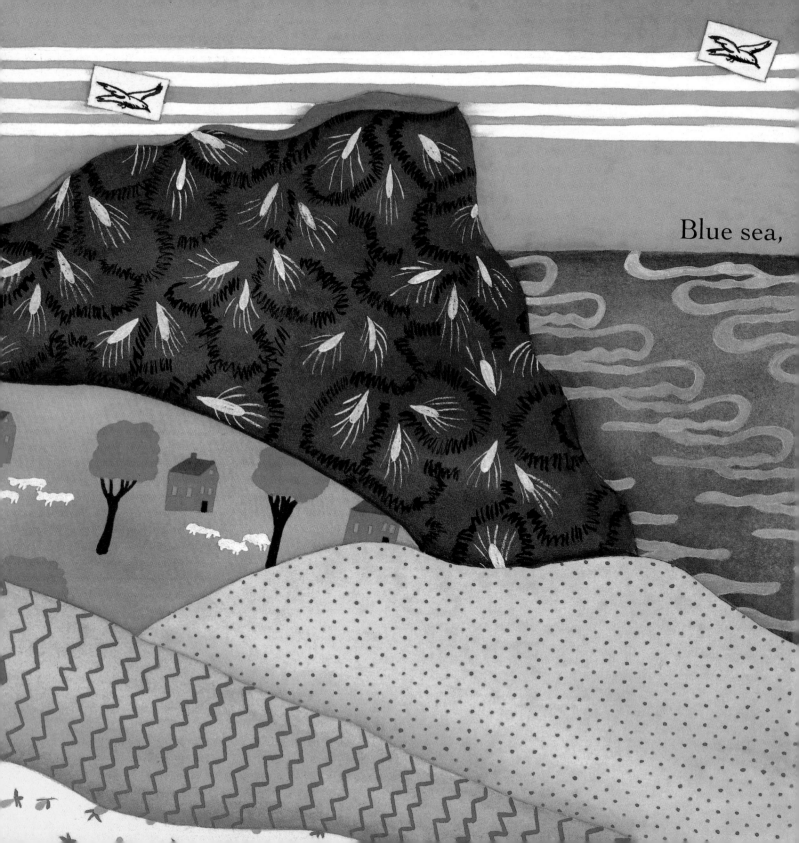

Blue sea,

blue sky too.

She put her needle down
and bit the thread.

"Come see what I have made,"
she said,
"of yellow, red and blue.

"A patchwork island, cut and sewed for you.
A place to play away long days
until the fields are mowed,
until the summer's through.

"And then
at night we'll use it as a quilt
to cover you in bed.

"These island nights can grow quite cool,"
she said.

The place I have written about in *Patchwork Island* is, in my mind, very specific—Prince Edward Island, Canada. It is very green, farmed with plowed fields and fields of crops running to the edge of the cliffs that drop to the sea. Rolling hills, dunes and sandy beaches skirt the water's edge. The cliffs and roads are red. The landscape is quilted by different greens of growth, the patterns of plow and crop. Here and there, stands of trees separate the fields. There are fishing villages and old houses, mostly clapboard, nothing fancy—barns with gambrel roofs, houses with one attic window looking out from beneath a peaked roof.

The little house I know best sits near the edge of a cliff looking out at the Gulf of St. Lawrence. To the left there is a freshwater pond and a cut that runs through the dunes to the sea. The Canada geese come by and drop down on our pond. The shags (cormorants) arrow by to their home on Shag Rock down the coast. We are at Park Corner; French River is down the road. Kensington and Summerside are the closest towns. When you look out to the horizon, the next stop is France.

—Karla Kuskin